D0971713

The little book of I love you

The little book of I love you

sacha goldberger

CHRONICLE BOOKS

SAN FRANCISCO

ISBN-10 0-8118-5362-4
ISBN-13 978-0-8118-5362-0

The Library of Congress has cataloged the previous edition as follows:

Goldberger, Sacha.
    [Petit livre de Je t'aime. English]
    The little book of I love you / Sacha Goldberger.
        p. cm.
    ISBN 2-02-063949-1
    1. Love—Quotations, maxims, etc. I. Title.
    PN6084.L6G65 2004
    302.3—dc22
                        2004056135

Cover design by John Brookson

Manufactured in China

10 9 8 7 6 5 4

Chronicle Books LLC
680 Second Street
San Francisco, California 94107

www.chroniclebooks.com

Foryouforeverlilimylove.

I get all choked up over you.

The water of life.

clouds head

Your love takes me higher.

Blinded by love.

youyouyouyouyouyou
youyouyouyouyouyou
youyouyouyouyouyou
youyouyouyouyouyou
youyouyouyouyouyou
youyouyouyouyouyou
youyouyouyouyouyou
youyou   I see you everywhere.   youyou
youyouyouyouyouyou
youyouyouyouyouyou
youyouyouyouyouyou
youyouyouyouyouyou
youyouyouyouyouyou
youyouyouyouyouyou
youyouyouyouyouyou

Cross my heart.

Loving you has made me bananas.

I love you squared.

I love you

plain and simple.

I love you

in Australia.

I love you

in Pisa.

I love you

in England.

I LOVE YOU

in Jerusalem.

in Paris.

My heart pounds for you.

heaven
heaven
heaven
heaven
heaven
heaven
heaven

Lines straight from my heart.

Love is priceless.

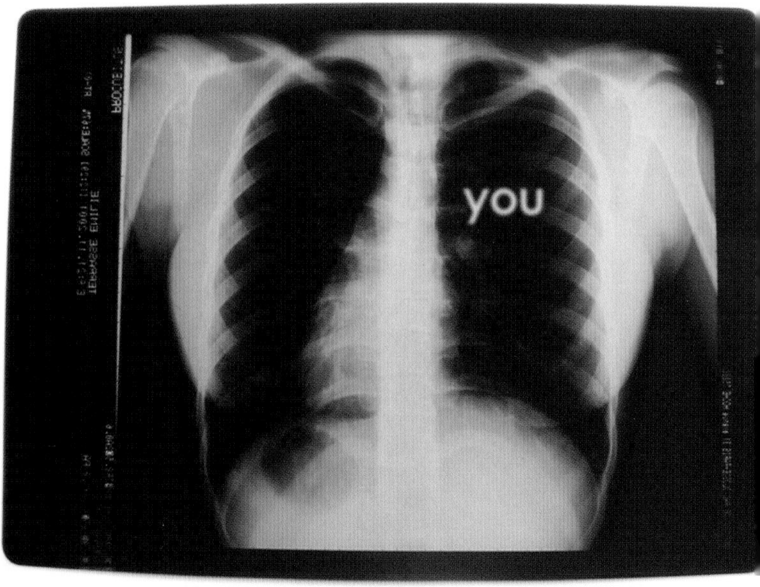
you

You make me lose focus.

me

You make my heart swell.

Connect the dots.

.28 .29
.27   .30 .2 .3 .4
.26   .1   .5
                         .6
.25   .7
                          .8
.24   .9
.23   .10
 .22   .11
 .21   .12
  .20
   .19   .13
    .18   .14
     .17   .15
       .16

The perfect pillow.

Say it with flowers.

You can count on me.

1 2 3 4 5 6 7 8 9
me

Me, once upon a time.

Head
Heels

I love you, .

In sickness and in health

I lub you

Only you allowed.

PRIVATE PROPERTY
NO TRESPASSING

my love for you can't be contained.

Just in case you get lost.

A toast to love.

If you were sad.

Let me whisper in your ear.

I love you

You butter my bread.

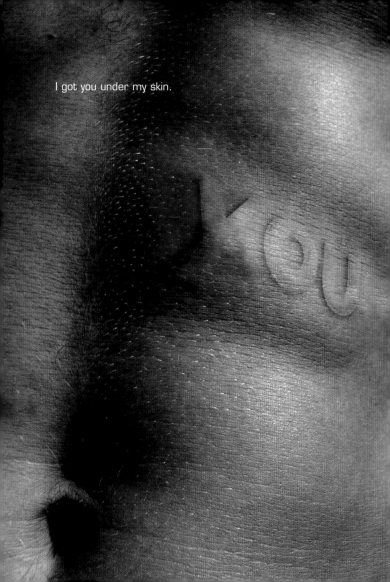

I got you under my skin.

You are my sunshine.

Please let it be you.

A message from my inner child.

A cheesy I love you.

A reflection of my feelings.

I love you

1 2 3 4 5 6 7 8 9 10 11 12 13 14 15 16 17 18
19 20 21 22 23 24 25 26 27 28 29 30 31 32
33 34 35 36 37 38 39 40 41 42 43 44 45 46
47 48 49 50 51 52 53 54 55 56 57 58 59 60
61 62 63 64 65 66 67 68 69 70 71 72 73 74
75 76 77 78 79 80 81 82 83 84 85 86 87 88
89 90 91 92 93 94 95 96 97 98 99 100 101
102 103 104 105 106 107 108 109 110 111
112 113 114 115 116 117 118 119 120121
122 123 124 125 126 127 128 129 130 131
132 133 134 135 136 137 138 139 140 141
142 143 144 145 146 147 148 149 150 151
152 153 154 155 156 157 158 159 160 161
162 163 164 165 166 167 168 169 170 171
172 173 174 175 176 177 178 179 180 181
182 183 184 185 186 187 188 189 190 191
192 193 194 195 196 197 198 199 200 201
202 203 204 205 206 207 208 209 210 211
212 213 214 215 216 217 218 219 220 221
222 223 224 225 226 227 228 229 230 231
232 233 234 235 236 237 238 239 240 241
242 243 244 245 246 247 248 249 250 251
252 253 254 255 256 257 258 259 260 261
262 263 264 265 266 267 268 269 270 271
272 273 274 275 276 ...   Let me count the ways.

You amaze me.

Sweetheart.

Parked in the red zone.

I love you

I can't disguise my love for you.

About you.

Always trust your first impression.

"G" spot hidden on this page.

G.

I love you

I can't keep my feelings in the dark.

Handle with care.

You give me fever.

Craving you.

I love you too.

You are intoxicating.

you   you

Love quickly developed.

How crosswalks should look.

head

I love you

toe toe toe toe toe toe toe toe toe toe

I'll love you forever.

Let me cover you with kisses.

naked

Yeeeeehaaaaaa!

www.lloveyou.com

I always knew we'd click.

Can you feel how much I love you?

Stuck on you.

you

An in-flight message.

I love you more and more.

I love you

You are one in a million.

FADE RESISTANT

An SOS to your heart.

.. .−..−−−...−. −.−− −−−..−

When you look at me.

Sheepish with love for you.

I love ewe

A color-blind I love you.

Only onion tears around here.

love all

Lucky I spotted you.

Add oil and apply to shoulders as needed.

There's an I love you hidden behind this cloud.

How I see the world when I'm with you.

You are the apple of my eye.

i love you

Target practice for Cupid.

A convenient excuse
to kiss under this book.

What I look like when you say I love you.

An I love you full of love.

I love you

An I love you to keep vampires at bay.

I love you in shorthand.

I lv u

Just a reminder.

A tarted-up I love you.

I love

Missing you.

You make me stumble over my words.

I lolove you

A shagadelic I love you.

You leave me speechless.

White hot.

Sending you my love.

A potato to say I love you.

In case of burning love.

An even better potato to say I love you.

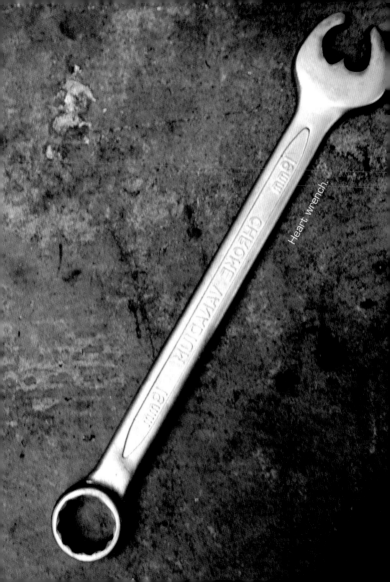

Heart wrench.

A stone to say the same thing that the potato said.

If Cupid upgraded to a paintgun.

Evergreen.

Love is in the air.

love

Splendor in the grass.

Will you be mine?

☐ yes
☐ yes

Put your
love's picture
here

For a big hug, quickly turn the page.

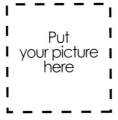

Side by side.

me you

Free trial, no obligation.